EINSTEIN IN 90 MINUTES

D0029135

In the same series by the same authors:

Halley in 90 minutes
Curie in 90 minutes
Darwin in 90 minutes

forthcoming titles

Faraday in 90 minutes
Galileo in 90 minutes
Mendel in 90 minutes
Newton in 90 minutes

John and Mary Gribbin

EINSTEIN
(1879–1955)
in 90 minutes

Constable · London

First published in Great Britain 1997
by Constable and Company Limited
3 The Lanchesters, 162 Fulham Palace Road
London W6 9ER
Copyright © John and Mary Gribbin 1997
The right of John and Mary Gribbin to be identified
as authors of this work has been asserted by them
in accordance with the Copyright,
Designs and Patents Act 1988
ISBN 0 09 477130 8
Set in Linotype Sabon by
Rowland Phototypesetting Ltd,
Bury St Edmunds, Suffolk
Printed in Great Britain by
St Edmundsbury Press Ltd,
Bury St Edmunds, Suffolk

A CIP catalogue record of this book
is available from the British Library

Contents

Einstein in context

At the end of the nineteenth century, physics had seemed on the verge of completion. Two great theories held sway. Isaac Newton's theory of gravity, combined with his laws of mechanics, explained how material objects move through the Universe, how planets orbit the Sun, how pendulums swing and how balls roll down inclined planes. Even the behaviour of gases, liquids and solids could be explained in terms of hard, indivisible atoms bouncing against one another like billiard balls and recoiling in accordance with Newton's laws.

The other great theory, developed only in the second half of the nineteenth century, was James Clerk Maxwell's theory of electromagnetism. In a set of just four equations, the greatest achievement of physics since the time of Newton himself, Maxwell had provided a complete description of all electric and magnetic phenomenon. It not only explained how two electrically charged balls repel or attract one another, and why a compass needle points north, but also interpreted the behaviour of light in terms of an electromagnetic wave, and predicted other forms of electromagnetic radiation, soon discovered and named radio waves.

It's worth emphasizing that gravity and electromagnetism were the only two basic types of forces that were known – indeed, the only two that anybody had any inkling existed – in the nineteenth century. So if you had a perfectly satisfactory theory of gravity, and a perfectly satisfactory theory of electromagnetism, plus a perfectly satisfactory set of laws of mechanics to describe how things like billiard-ball atoms or the pendulum of a clock moved, what more did you need? For example, any physicist who wanted to work out how the pressure of gas in a sealed chamber would change because the temperature changed (a very useful thing to be able to do in the era of steam-driven industry) could do so using these known laws of physics. Anyone who wanted to work out the details of laying a telegraph cable across the Atlantic seabed to establish a communications link between Europe and America (the original electronic superhighway) could do so with the aid of Maxwell's equations, confident that it would work and provide a good return on the investment. Indeed, Maxwell himself made a fortune from the patents on just such a transatlantic cable. And it is still true today that just about everything we encounter in the everyday physical world, the world of common sense, can be described entirely adequately in terms of the two great theories of Newton and Maxwell, plus Newton's laws of mechanics.

Things started to fall apart when physicists began to probe outward from the world of common sense, in both directions. In the mid-1890s they discovered that the atom is not indivisible, after all: J.J. Thomson, in Cambridge, chipped bits off it and named the bits electrons. And there were some odd puzzles about the behaviour of light. One was the question of *how* light travelled as a wave. The obvious analogy is with ripples on a pond, but there it is the water that moves to make the ripples. What is doing the 'waving' when a light wave passes by?

For a time, physicists seriously believed in the existence of something called the aether, which filled the entire Universe and provided the medium for light to travel through (by the way, when physicists talk of 'light', they mean any kind of electromagnetic radiation). If the Universe were filled with the aether, it would have to be a very tenuous sort of stuff in order to allow the Earth and other bodies to pass through it unimpeded. On the other hand, the speed of a wave through a medium (such as sound in air) increases as the stiffness and density of the medium increase. Sound travels through a bar of steel faster than it does through the air. Since the speed of light is very high (300 million metres per second), the aether would have to be incredibly stiff and unyielding to allow light waves to travel at such a speed.

On top of that, a series of extraordinarily careful measurements carried out by A.A. Michelson and Edward Morley in the 1880s failed to find any evidence that the speed of light varies according to whether the Earth is moving 'upstream' or 'downstream' through the aether. Indeed, there was no evidence at all that the aether existed. At the end of the nineteenth century many scientists were worried about this absence of evidence for the aether, but Einstein was not one of them. As we shall see, he arrived at his special theory of relativity from a different jumping-off point. He later said that at the time he developed that theory he had not heard of the Michelson–Morley experiment.

The last and, as it turned out, the most profound puzzle concerned the interaction of light and matter. The theory of light worked perfectly (except for the puzzle about the aether); the theory of matter worked perfectly (as far as it had been tested, a hundred years ago). But the theory of how matter, in the form of atoms, actually produced light did not work at all. It was obvious to physicists in the 1890s that, just as you can make ripples on a pond by wiggling your fingers about in the water, the electromagnetic waves that make up light must be produced by vibrations, or oscillations, of electrically charged entities within atoms (so they welcomed the discovery of electrons). But the 'classical' mechanics of Newton said that in such circumstances the charged entities should radiate away enormous amounts of energy very suddenly at very short wavelengths, in the blue and ultraviolet part of the spectrum. This was known as the 'ultraviolet catastrophe'. It was circumvented, right at the end of the nineteenth century, by Max Planck, who, more in despair than anything else, suggested that light could be emitted only in lumps of a certain size, which he called quanta. This prevented atoms radiating as much ultraviolet light as Newtonian mechanics would have allowed, and (rather artificially) gave an equation describing the emission of light (now known as the black-body curve) which matched the observations.

But though Planck had offered the idea of light being radiated in discrete quanta, he still thought of light purely as a wave phenomenon. In 1900, nobody at all thought that light really existed in little packets – as particles, now called photons. And that is where Albert Einstein came on the scene.

Life and work

Einstein was born in Ulm, in Germany, on 14 March 1879. He didn't stay there long, for in the early summer of 1880 the family moved to Munich, where Albert's father, Hermann, hoped to establish a successful business. Hermann had already run an unsuccessful electrochemical enterprise in Ulm, bankrolled by the parents of his wife, Pauline. It was Hermann's younger brother, Jakob, who suggested the move to Munich in search of success, and Jakob became a partner in the business. He lived with Hermann, Pauline and young Albert in a large house with a pleasant garden on the outskirts of Munich.

Albert was a quiet baby, and his parents became concerned as he seemed a little backward, and slow to learn to speak. But when he did start to talk, he did not babble in the way that babies usually do, but could be seen quietly constructing proper sentences in his head, his lips moving, before he uttered the words. In November 1881, when Albert was still a few months short of his 3rd birthday, his sister Maja was born, and the best picture we have of his early life comes from her reminiscences, now in the Einstein archive at Princeton University. Maja recalled her mother later telling how Albert had been promised something new to play with, but hadn't quite understood what was going on. When Maja was presented to him, his grumpy response was, 'Where are the wheels?' He had been expecting a new toy.

The relationship between brother and sister was close, but often tempestuous. In childhood, though by and large quiet and contemplative, Albert had a violent temper, and when roused would hurl the nearest object at the nearest person, usually Maja. On one occasion he smashed her over the head with a garden hoe. The tantrum that ensued when Pauline decided it was time for Albert to learn the violin frightened off his first teacher, but she soon found one with stronger nerves, and the agonies Albert went through in being forced to learn the instrument against his will were compensated for by his love of the violin throughout the rest of his life.

Hermann and Pauline encouraged what today seems an extraordinary degree of independence in their children from an early age. When he was no more than 4, Albert was not just allowed but encouraged to make his own way through the streets of their Munich suburb. A year later, two important events occurred in his life. First, he started attending school, which he hated. Although they were a Jewish family, the Einsteins were not particularly religious, and for convenience Albert was sent to a nearby Catholic school. The school believed in the old-fashioned method of rote learning, and enforced this with the traditional discipline of a rap over the knuckles (literally) for mistakes.

The second big event, when he was 5, both provided Albert with an escape (at least in his mind) from the school routine and, in the long term, reinforced his conviction that he was better off working things out for himself. When he was in bed with an illness, his father gave him a magnetic compass to help keep him amused. The young Einstein was fascinated by the instrument, and the way in which, no matter how it was turned, the needle always kept pointing north. The discovery that there was a mysterious force, which acted mysteriously on the compass needle, made a deep and lasting impression on him. Why hadn't anything as exciting and interesting as this been shown to him in school?

When he was 10, Einstein enrolled at the Luitpold *Gymnasium* (high school). By then, he had already discovered a love for mathematics, largely through the influence of his uncle Jakob and a young medical student, Max Talmud, who joined the family for supper every Thursday (it was then a tradition among middle-class Jewish families to help young students). Talmud discussed the latest scientific ideas with Albert as if he were an equal, and his uncle Jakob introduced him to algebra. When Einstein was 12, Talmud gave him a book about geometry; Einstein later described this as the single most important factor in turning him into a scientist.

It was just as well that he had these influences at home, because, after an initially bright start at the *Gymnasium* (though he had disliked the Catholic school, he had usually been near the top of the class), Einstein's grades had slipped as he lost interest in the rigid system and the dull teaching. More than one teacher commented that he was a wastrel who would never amount to anything. (This is not surprising, of course; what *would* be surprising would be to find any former high school student who hadn't been described by at least one teacher as a wastrel who would never amount to anything.)

The academic problems were brought to a head when the family faced another financial crisis as a result of Hermann's lack of business acumen. In 1894, Hermann was persuaded by Jakob that the future would be brighter in Italy, and the Einsteins sold up and moved south. But as Albert was at a crucial stage of his education, it was decided that he should stay behind, attending the *Gymnasium* and living in a nearby boarding-house. Although a relative was given the job of keeping a watchful eye on Albert (he was only just 15), this is another example of the way in which Hermann and Pauline encouraged their children to be independent, undoubtedly a factor in the way Einstein sailed through life largely unconcerned about domestic comforts or social niceties.

Einstein was concerned, though, about the tedium of living alone and spending his days in boredom induced by the German educational system. Within six months, he managed to convince the family doctor that the situation was so dreadful that he was on the brink of a nervous breakdown, and was given a letter to that effect, which he took to his maths teacher. This was one of the few teachers at all sympathetic to his plight (since Albert was one of his best students, it was easy to be sympathetic), and he provided the would-be drop-out with a letter saying that there was nothing more he could teach the boy. Armed with these documents, Einstein confronted the principal of the *Gymnasium* and announced that he was leaving for medical reasons. The principal replied that, on the contrary, young Albert was hereby expelled. Either way, Einstein left the school and headed south to join his family in Pavia.

There was another reason for his eagerness to leave Germany. Had he stayed until he was 17, he would have been obliged to do a year's military service, a prospect which the now pacifist Einstein, who loathed any form of discipline or authority, dreaded. Whatever his motives in leaving Munich – and whatever the doctor's letter said – he showed no signs of an incipient nervous breakdown when he turned up, unannounced, in Pavia. Maja describes him as being in high spirits. He renounced his German citizenship, clearly an act announcing his newfound freedom, and persuaded his father to let him spend months touring the art centres of Italy before settling down to any serious work (perhaps the doctor's letter came in handy here). But when the rest cure was over, Einstein fought long and hard with his father about his future.

Albert had a rather vague notion that he might become a teacher of philosophy; Hermann wanted him to get practical qualifications and help in the family business. Either way, he would at least need to get a college diploma, and under parental pressure Albert applied for admission to the prestigious Federal Institute of Technology, in Zurich (the Eidgenössische Technische Hochschule, or ETH).

Einstein set off to take the entrance examination to the ETH in the autumn of 1895. He was still six months short of his 17th birthday, and the normal age for admission was 18. Even so, the confident (some would say arrogant) teenager was shocked when he failed the exam. He scored very well in science and mathematics, but not well enough in languages, history, literature and art to qualify. But the authorities took account of his relative youth, and told him that if he enrolled at a Swiss school and obtained the standard high school diploma, he would be admitted the following year without having to take the examination again.

For this compulsory year back in school, Einstein really fell on his feet. A friend of Hermann Einstein recommended a small country school in Aarau, where conditions were relaxed and Albert was happy. Even better, he boarded with Professor Jost Winteler, the principal of the school, and the professor's daughter, Marie, became Albert's first sweetheart. Although that relationship did not survive when Einstein moved on to the ETH, the family connection did – Albert's sister Maja later married Marie's brother, Paul.

Einstein sailed through his diploma examination in the early autumn of 1896, with perfect marks for history, geometry, descriptive geometry and physics, a mere 80 per cent for German, Italian, chemistry and natural history, and 60 per cent for geography, art and technical drawing. He arrived in Zurich on 29 October 1896, ready to start his new life.

Being a university student was the ideal life for Einstein. He went to the lectures he liked, and didn't bother with the rest (the vast majority). He read what he liked, dressed how he liked, and spent a lot of time in cafés and bars, discussing with his friends the meaning of life, or the latest ideas in physics. Famously, one of his teachers, Hermann Minkowski (who, unusually, Einstein had great respect for) described him as 'a lazy dog who never bothered about mathematics at all.'

There were only five students (including Einstein) taking the science course in Einstein's year at the ETH, and one of them was a woman, Mileva Maric. It was typical of Einstein that he was the one among the four male students in the group who established a close relationship with Mileva, for he always liked the company of women. Thrown into close proximity with just one woman in an otherwise male group, it was perhaps inevitable that a relationship would develop. He had other female friends, but during his last year at the ETH, 1899/1900, the relationship with Mileva became a full-blown love affair. They talked of marriage but knew that this would be opposed by Albert's mother, who would not think her son ready for married life.

First, though, they had to get their final examinations out of the way. Belatedly, Einstein realized that it might have been wise to spend at least some time studying the official syllabuses. He borrowed the lecture notes of his more diligent friend, Marcel Grossman, and mugged up furiously. To the surprise of nobody but himself, he achieved the lowest scores of the four students who graduated from the course on 28 July 1900. Just one person did even worse than him, and failed – Mileva.

The combination of Einstein's scraped pass and the cavalier way in which he had treated his studies now left him with real problems in finding a job. The lecturers at the ETH were certainly not inclined to offer him a position as an assistant at the polytechnic (the usual way for a young scientist to embark on an academic career), nor were they likely to give him a glowing reference. He intended to carry out research on his own, including a thesis that would lead to the award of a Ph.D. from the University of Zurich. This would be no problem. He was full of ideas, and as a theorist the only equipment he needed was pencil and paper, and access to a good library. Even library access wasn't that important, for Einstein always worked out problems from first principles for himself, often in deliberate ignorance of previous attempts. But it would be necessary to make a living of some kind while studying science in his spare time.

Then there was the problem of Mileva. She decided to retake her final year at the ETH and sit the examinations again. Several months before the examinations, she found she was pregnant. Unmarried, with no prospects, and with Albert also without prospects, it is hardly surprising that she could not concentrate on her studies, and she failed the exam again. By the end of 1901, though

Albert had found temporary work as a teacher, things looked very bleak for the couple. The first chink of light came through the efforts of Marcel Grossman. Having been instrumental in getting Einstein through his degree, Grossman now persuaded his father, who was a friend of the Director of the Swiss Patent Office in Berne, to use his influence to help Einstein secure a job there.

This famous job did not actually materialize until June 1902. In the meantime, Mileva, who had gone into seclusion with her parents, gave birth to Einstein's illegitimate daughter, Lieserl, at the end of January. News of the baby, and Einstein's relationship with Mileva, would have killed his prospects of the desperately needed job, and probably for this reason the baby was soon given up for adoption, and never heard of again.

Einstein stayed at the Patent Office from June 1902 until July 1909, long after he had made a name for himself as a scientist, and after he had begun to receive offers of academic posts. Clearly the work suited him. His keen mind was quickly able to find the flaws in patent applications, leaving him time to think about physics even during office hours. Although Einstein was saddened by the death of his father in the Autumn of 1902, in the wake of this loss Pauline withdrew her objections to Albert's marriage to Mileva, which took place on 6 January 1903. The young patent officer now had a respectable family life, with Mileva increasingly cast in the conventional domestic role of housewife. For intellectual company he had his own circle of friends, notably Maurice Solovine, Conrad Habicht and Michelangelo Besso, who mockingly referred to themselves as the 'Olympia Academy' and discussed new ideas in physics, providing a sounding-board for Einstein as he developed a breathtaking series of ideas in just a few short years.

Einstein had several scientific papers published in the early years of the twentieth century, seemingly unhampered by his lack of an academic position. None was spectacular, but all were solid pieces of work. One of the recurrent themes of these early works was his attempt to establish the physical reality of atoms and molecules, which was still a matter for debate at that time. This project was the motivation behind Einstein's Ph.D. thesis, which he completed in 1905.

In his thesis, Einstein calculated the way in which molecules in solution behave. The specific molecules he studied were those of sugar, dissolved in water – essentially, his calculations apply to the behaviour of hot, sweet tea. By calculating the way in which the sugar molecules ought to exert a pressure within the liquid, and comparing this with experimental data, Einstein worked out the size of a sugar molecule to be just over a millionth of a centimetre across. This was an extremely accurate estimate by the standards of the day, and certainly good enough to justify the award of the Ph.D. There was only one snag. When Einstein submitted the thesis to the University of Zurich on 20 July 1905 (he had actually finished it in April), he was told that the science was fine, but the thesis was too short. In later years he took great delight in recounting how he added one sentence to the thesis before resubmitting it, whereupon it was promptly accepted!

Einstein may have delayed submitting the thesis simply because he was so busy between

April and July 1905. His fertile brain didn't stop working when the thesis was finished – on the contrary, there was an outpouring of papers on topics he had been holding back on while finishing the thesis. And all this was written while he was still holding down the day job at the Patent Office!

On 11 May, his paper on Brownian motion arrived at the offices of the German physics journal *Annalen der Physik*. Brownian motion is a strange, zigzag motion of tiny particles (such as pollen grains) suspended in a liquid or floating in the air. In the second half of the nineteenth century, several physicists had suggested that it might be caused by the particles being bombarded by molecules of air or water. But most of them missed a trick by guessing that each zig (or zag) was caused by the collision of a single molecule with the pollen grain, which would mean that molecules were comparable in size to the grains.

Einstein showed how the effect would arise from a constant, but uneven, bombardment by many tiny molecules, the size of the ones he had studied for his thesis. If a pollen grain is being bombarded on all sides, but the bombardment is slightly stronger from one direction, it will move accordingly. Crucially, Einstein put precise numbers into his calculations, describing the zigzag Brownian motion in rigorous statistical terms. It was the mathematical rigour of this paper that persuaded most physicists that Brownian motion is indeed caused by the dance of the molecules.

This paper is mentioned here because it follows on closely from the thesis work. In fact, though, it was the second of Einstein's papers to appear in the *Annalen der Physik* that year. The first one had been sent to them in March 1905, while he was in the midst of writing up his thesis and, of course, working by day in the Patent Office. Put like that, it sounds like an aside, a minor piece of work. Perhaps Einstein thought about it that way. Nevertheless, it was for this paper, on the photoelectric effect, that Einstein would later be awarded the Nobel prize for physics.

The experiments that Einstein explained in this work had been carried out in 1902 by the Hungarian researcher Philipp Lenard. Lenard studied how electrons are knocked out of a metal surface by light – the photoelectric effect. He found that for light with a certain colour, all the electrons 'boiled off' in this way carry the same amount of energy. If the light is brighter, more electrons are liberated but each of them has the same energy. But if you change the colour of the light, you change the energy carried off by each electron.

Einstein's explanation (again, backed up by rigorous maths) was that the light quanta invoked by Planck to resolve the ultraviolet catastrophe that arose in the context of black-body radiation should be regarded as real particles. He said that in the photoelectric effect one electron is knocked out of the metal surface by one of the light particles (now called photons). A brighter beam of light just has more photons in it, but each photon still has the same energy. So the energy carried off by each electron is equal to the energy of the photon that liberated the electron. All photons of the same colour have the same energy, but photons with different colours have different energies. This explained Lenard's observations.

At the time, this paper made very little impact. Physicists were happy with the idea of light as a wave, and largely dismissed the notion that it could be a stream of particles. It was only later that the idea of 'wave-particle duality', which says that in the subatomic world an entity such as a photon or an electron has to be regarded as both wave *and* particle, became a cornerstone of the new quantum physics.

Jumping ahead a little, it is amusing to see how people's minds were changed, and Einstein got his Nobel prize. The American physicist Robert Millikan was so annoyed by Einstein's suggestion, and so convinced that light was nothing but a wave, that he carried out a series of superb experiments with the express intention of proving Einstein wrong. He succeeded only in proving that Einstein was right – and, being a good scientist, he accepted the evidence and changed his tune. Late in life, looking back on those years, Millikan commented:

I spent ten years of my life testing that 1905 equation of Einstein's and contrary to all my expectations, I was compelled in 1915 to assert its unambiguous verification in spite of its unreasonableness.

It must have been some consolation to Millikan that he received his Nobel prize for physics, partly for this work, in 1923. Einstein had received his prize, for the photoelectric effect, in 1922 (actually the 1921 prize, held over for a year), and the citation specifically mentioned Millikan's work.

Back in 1905, though, Einstein still hadn't finished. Yet another paper arrived in the offices of the *Annalen der Physik* on 30 June (still several weeks before the thesis was submitted!). This one dealt with the behaviour of light, and the 'electrodynamics' of moving objects. It introduced to the world the special theory of relativity.

The jumping-off point for the special theory ('special' here means 'restricted', because the theory deals only with objects moving at constant speeds in straight lines, not the more general case of accelerations) was the way in which Maxwell's equations give a unique value for the speed of light. In the old Newtonian picture, if you stood still and shone a beam of light, travelling at 300 million metres per second, towards a spaceship hurtling towards you at 100 million metres per second, the crew of the spaceship would expect to measure the speed of light in the beam as 400 million metres per second. But there is nothing in Maxwell's equations to allow for this possibility. They say that they, too, should measure the speed of light in the beam at 300 million metres per second.

Anybody who thought much about this in the early years of the twentieth century assumed that there was something wrong with Maxwell's theory, since Newton's ideas were sacrosanct. It is a mark of Einstein's independence of mind that he was willing to consider the possibility that Maxwell was right and Newton was wrong. It is also a mark of his flexibility of mind that he developed these ideas, using the wave theory of light, in the same year that he proved light to be a stream of particles. Einstein was, in fact, the first person to take on board the idea of wave–particle duality, as the quantum pioneer Niels Bohr always acknowledged.

Everything in the special theory is built (with due mathematical rigour) upon this one foundation – that the speed of light is an absolute constant, the same for all observers, regardless of how they are moving or how the source of the light is moving. The equations then show unequivocally that moving objects shrink and gain in mass, and moving clocks run slow. It is literally true that, for example, time runs more slowly (by a tiny fraction!) inside a moving aeroplane than it does for those of us on the ground. If you travelled in a fast spaceship to another star and back, your journey might seem to you to take a few months, but you would return to find that many years had passed on Earth.

There is no need here to go into the details of the equations. But it is important to stress that all the predictions of the special theory have been tried and tested in hundreds of experiments. They even form part of engineering practice: when engineers build particle accelerators like those at CERN, the European research laboratory in Geneva, they have to take account of relativistic effects in order to get the beams of particles to move in the way the physicists want. These are multi-million dollar, international projects. If the special theory were wrong, those accelerators wouldn't work, and a lot of politicians would want to know why.

Shortly after Einstein had sent off his paper on the special theory, he had a kind of afterthought. He realized that the special theory implied a connection between mass and energy, making them equivalent to one another. The afterthought appeared in the *Annalen der Physik* in November 1905, two months after the main paper on the special theory, and introduced the most famous equation in all of science: $E = mc^2$, where E is the energy stored in an object with mass m, and c is the speed of light. At the time, hardly anybody took any notice of either of these papers.

The background to all this intellectual activity was a settled home life, in which Mileva seemed happy with her domestic role. The couple's second child (and first to be openly acknowledged), Hans Albert, was born on 14 May 1904. In September that year, Albert's annual salary was increased from 3,500 to 3,900 francs, and though not wealthy the Einsteins were able to take holidays, and Albert took up a new hobby, sailing. In the world outside the family circle this was a time of optimism and vitality. In 1905, Franz Lehar wrote *The Merry Widow*, and H.G. Wells wrote *Kipps*; in 1900, the first Kodak Box Brownie had been produced. While Einstein was starting to revolutionize physics in Switzerland, the first electric tram appeared on the streets of London. In a darker hint of things to come, in the year that Einstein published his first relativity papers there was an unsuccessful revolution in Russia.

Although the special theory itself made the least immediate impact of Einstein's great 1905 papers, the whole body of work he produced that year began to make his name known. There were no more significant papers for several years, though Einstein did continue to publish. In April 1906, soon after his 27th birthday, he was promoted to technical expert (second class) in the Patent Office, with a rise in salary to 4,500 francs a year. But friends began to urge him to find an academic post, and to recommend him to the relevant authorities.

It was a slow process. The first rung on the academic ladder would be a position as a *Privatdozent*, an unpaid lecturer who was nevertheless an official member of a university, and could give lectures on a subject of his choice, charging students a fee to attend. In 1907, Einstein applied for just such a post at Berne University, but was turned down – partly because the papers on the special theory, included in the package supporting his application, were described as 'incomprehensible' by the head of the physics department there. Wounded, Einstein considered several jobs in teaching over the next few months, but nothing came of them. In 1908, however, he was at last appointed as a *Privatdozent* at Berne. There was no question of giving up his now well-paid job at the Patent Office on the strength of such a modest position, and Einstein's first lectures as a member of the University, delivered in the winter of 1908/9, were given on Saturday and Tuesday mornings, from 7 to 8 a.m. Hardly surprisingly, they were not well attended. Progress up the academic ladder might therefore still have been slow, in spite of Einstein's growing reputation. But just at this point his career received a crucial boost, though he did not at first appreciate it. It came, ironically, from Hermann Minkowski, the professor at the ETH who just a few years previously had described Einstein as a 'lazy dog'.

In 1902, Minkowski had become Professor of Mathematics at Göttingen University, where he stayed for the rest of his career. He was one of the first to appreciate the importance of the special theory of relativity, and he took the crucial step of linking Einstein's mathematical description of space and time into a geometrical description, the four-dimensional spacetime. In a lecture delivered in Cologne on 2 September 1908 (it was published in 1909), Minkowski (who *was* familiar with the Michelson–Morley experiment) introduced the idea of time as the fourth dimension with the following words:

The views of space and time which I wish to lay before you have sprung from the soil of experimental physics, and therein lies their strength. They are radical. Henceforth space by itself, and time by itself, are doomed to fade away into mere shadows, and only a kind of union of the two will preserve an independent reality.

Einstein was not immediately impressed with Minkowski's geometrization of his theory, which he saw as an unnecessary mathematical trick. But it was Minkowski's variation on the theme of the special theory that made its importance clear to a wide audience, and Einstein eventually got to like it – not least because it would point the way for his own greatest work.

It is no coincidence that soon after Minkowski's lecture had been published, Einstein at last obtained a paid academic appointment, as Professor of Physics at the University of Zurich, in 1909. He resigned from the Patent Office on 6 July, and never looked back. Before long, instead of him seeking employment at any university that would have him, a succession of universities would fight for his services as the most prestigious scientific name to have associated with their physics department.

But before he left the Patent Office, day-dreaming about physics at his desk one day in 1907, Einstein had experienced what he later described as 'the happiest thought' of his life – the idea that a falling person cannot feel their own weight. Weight is caused by gravity: it is the force we feel because of the Earth tugging on us. A falling person is accelerating under the influence of gravity (in free fall), but feels no weight. This is why a fall never hurt anybody; what hurts is the sudden end to the fall, when the ground gets in the way. The acceleration precisely cancels out the weight, an insight which showed Einstein that gravity and acceleration are equivalent to one another. If he could extend his theory of relativity to the general case, to include acceleration, he would automatically have a theory of gravity as well!

It took eight years from that happy thought for Einstein to achieve this goal (longer than the time from when he graduated to when he had the happy thought), but he got there in the end. During those years he became a father for the third time, when Eduard was born on 28 July 1910. He moved several times, achieving a higher academic status at every step: in 1911 he moved to Prague; in 1912, back to Zurich as a Professor at the ETH, from which he had graduated so ingloriously; and in the spring of 1914 to Berlin.

This was a top job, almost on terms dictated by Einstein to a university desperate to recruit him. Germany was then the centre of physics, and the offer was irresistible, though with hindsight Einstein might have been happier if he had stayed in Switzerland. The frequent moves were not at all to Mileva's taste, and as Einstein's prestige grew the marriage began to fall apart. After only a brief time in Berlin she left, taking the children back to Switzerland with her.

In Berlin, Einstein had the freedom and the time to complete his masterwork, but no domestic support. Everything was being changed by the First World War. Living on his own in wartime Berlin, sending most of his money to Switzerland to support his family, and working furiously on what became the general theory of relativity, Einstein seriously neglected his bodily needs. He wasn't quite alone in Berlin. His divorced cousin Elsa and her two daughters lived nearby, and kept an eye on him. (Indeed, it was partly suspicion about just how affectionate the relationship between Einstein and his cousin was that made Mileva so reluctant to move to Berlin in the first place, and so unhappy when she got there.)

It was just as well they did keep an eye. One of Elsa's daughters, Margot, later told how one day in the autumn of 1915, when Einstein was working almost round the clock to complete his new theory, she called on him and found him boiling an egg (which he hadn't bothered to wash, even though it was fresh from the farm with sundry unsavoury items stuck to it) in a pan of soup to save time, intending to stuff them both down his throat as quickly as possible to provide the fuel his body needed to get on with the job. Hardly surprizingly, living like this he lost weight and suffered agonizing bouts of what was assumed to be indigestion.

From Einstein's point of view, it was all

worth it. He found the way to generalize his theory of space and time, extending it to include acceleration and gravity, and he presented the masterwork to the Prussian Academy of Sciences in Berlin in a series of three lectures in November 1915. The general theory was published in 1916, and almost immediately Einstein applied it to describe mathematically the entirety of space and time, the Universe at large.

The general theory of relativity is a highly mathematical theory, and you need at least a degree in maths to get to grips with the equations. But thanks to Minkowski's geometrization of spacetime, it is relatively easy to get a mental picture of what it is all about.

The key insight stems from the idea of a falling lift, with a beam of light shone across it. Because the lift is in free fall, the occupants feel as if they are floating in space. In a freely floating lift the light beam would cross the lift in a straight line. So, Einstein reasoned, it must do the same in the falling lift. But to an outside observer (imagine, now, that the walls of the lift are made of glass) the path of the light beam would appear curved as it dipped to keep up with the downward acceleration of the lift on its way from one side to the other. If the lift fell past the light beam and left it behind, as common sense seems to dictate, the observers inside the lift would know that they are falling – but they don't. The light beam, though, doesn't 'know' whether the lift is there or not, when it is halfway across. So it must behave in the same way regardless of whether the lift is there or not; and, Einstein reasoned, it is being bent by gravity, the same gravity responsible for the acceleration of the lift. But how?

This is where the image of spacetime comes in. We cannot picture four dimensions, so physicists often ignore two of the dimensions of space (after all, all three of these dimensions behave in the same way) and imagine a stretched rubber sheet as representing a two-dimensional world in which one dimension is space and the other is time. A flat sheet like this corresponds to the state of spacetime far from any matter. A marble rolled across the sheet represents a light beam travelling in a straight line.

Now dump a heavy object, like a bowling

ball, on the stretched rubber sheet. It makes a dent. A marble rolled near the bowling ball will follow a curved path around the dent. If it moves slowly, it will fall right into the dent; the faster it moves, the more nearly its path is a straight line, but it is always curved to some extent. The trajectory of a fast-moving marble represents a light beam bent by gravity. In other words, curved space tells matter how to move, and the presence of matter tells space how to curve. But the really neat thing about Einstein's new theory was that it predicted, with great mathematical precision, exactly how much space should be curved, and therefore how much light should be bent, near a massive object like the Sun.

News of Einstein's ideas travelled from wartime Berlin to neutral Holland, where Willem de Sitter passed them on to the eminent astronomer Arthur Eddington, in wartime London. It just happened that there was to be an eclipse of the Sun on 29 May 1919. If the war had finished by then, Eddington realized, this would be an ideal opportunity to test the theory. During an eclipse, stars visible close to the edge of the Sun can be photographed, and their positions in the photographs can be compared with ones taken of the same part of the sky six months earlier, at night, when the Sun was on the other side of the Earth. If Einstein was correct the light-bending effect should shift the positions of the stars in the eclipse photographs by a tiny but precisely predictable amount. There was one snag – the 1919 eclipse would not be visible from Europe, and an expedition would have to be mounted to take the crucial photographs from the island of Principe, off the western coast of Africa. That is why the war would have to end first.

The war did finish on time, the photographs were taken and (though it took months for the photographs to be brought back to Britain and analyzed) Einstein's theory was soon declared triumphant. In the aftermath of war (technically still during the war, since in May 1919 the formal peace treaty had yet to be signed) the prediction of a German theorist (as he was perceived; in fact Einstein was a Swiss citizen at that time) had been confirmed by a British astronomer. The news broke on 6 November 1919, when

the results from Eddington's eclipse
expedition were announced at a joint meeting
of the Royal Society and the Royal Astro-
nomical Society in London. This token of a
hoped-for reconciliation between warring
nations helped to boost public interest in the
news to heights usually reserved these days
for stories about pop stars or lapsed royal
princesses, and, at the age of 40, Einstein
became world-famous overnight.

But the Einstein who became world-famous
in 1919 was, in many ways, not the Einstein
who had achieved the breakthrough in 1915.
The years of neglect had taken their toll on
his body. After completing the general theory
and his early work on cosmology, Einstein
collapsed. The indigestion turned out to be
an ulcer, and in two months Einstein lost
about 25 kilos in weight. As well as the physical illness he seems to have suffered a serious
nervous breakdown. During the second half
of 1917 he was largely bedridden, looked
after by Elsa and her daughters (Margot was
now 18, her sister Ilse 20), who brought him
hot meals. This wasn't as easy as it sounds.
Because of the Allied blockade, food was

scarce in Berlin, and without someone to care for him in this way it is hard to see how Einstein would have survived. In the late summer of 1917, he moved to an apartment in the same block as Elsa and her daughters, and it was only in the spring of 1918, almost a year after becoming ill, that he was able to leave the house.

Einstein certainly needed someone to look after him, and Elsa was happy to make the relationship permanent. Indeed, by the summer of 1918 she was anxious to put their relationship on a respectable footing – she was after all concerned about her reputation, with Einstein living under the same roof, if not yet technically in the same apartment. Mileva agreed, reluctantly, to a divorce; the details were sorted out by Einstein's old friend, Besso, acting as intermediary. One of the conditions was that she would receive the financial part of Einstein's yet-to-be-awarded Nobel prize, which all of them confidently expected would be awarded soon. This was neither arrogance nor prescience; Einstein had been nominated for the award almost every year since 1910, and he can hardly have been unaware of this. The Nobel committee kept on choosing other people, largely because they were baffled by Einstein's work, but most physicists felt that an award to Einstein was already overdue, and sooner or later the committee would have to see reason. The prize, amounting to about 30,000 Swedish kronor at the time, would be enough to provide a modestly comfortable standard of living for Mileva and the two boys.

The divorce was finalized in February 1919, and Einstein married Elsa (who was three years his senior) in June, just as he was about to become famous outside the world of science. Even his physical appearance had changed as a result of his illness. Five years earlier, as photographs show, he was a young-looking man with a mass of dark hair; in the summer of 1919, he looked older than his 40 years, with the shock of grey hair (soon turning white) that was to become his trademark. In the public mind, Albert Einstein will always be the wise old man of science, a figure who could easily stand in for the popular image of God. But this sometimes conceals the fact that most of his great work was carried out as an active young man, with dashing good looks, an eye for the ladies, and a love of cafés and bars. After hc became famous, and was under the protective wing of Elsa, nothing would ever be quite the same again.

One of the most astonishing things about Einstein the scientist, though, was that even in his forties, with a serious physical and mental breakdown behind him and global fame to cope with, he was not finished. He was to make one more lasting contribution to physics, at an age when most scientists are long past their 'best before' date.

Einstein had maintained his interest in the nature of light quanta – photons – after his work on the photoelectric effect in 1905. In 1916, just after completing the general theory and not long before his breakdown, he had made another major contribution to the understanding of the interaction between light and matter. In this he explained how electrons jumping from one energy level inside an atom to another energy level (in the same atom) could emit or absorb photons. Among other things, these results predicted that if an atom is already in a suitable high-energy state, then the passage of a photon with the right energy (the right colour) would trigger the atom to release an identical photon. It is this 'stimulated emission of radiation' that is the basis of the laser.

From 1919 to 1924 Einstein was not very productive, by his own previous standards. He travelled the world as a guest lecturer, visiting many countries in Europe and travelling farther afield to the United States, Palestine and Japan. Everywhere he went he picked up awards (including, as we have mentioned, the Nobel prize – eventually). When he was at home, the turmoil in Germany following the First World War gave him plenty to worry about. But in the summer of 1924 Einstein's last great burst of scientific activity was triggered by the arrival of a communication from a young Indian researcher, Satyendra Bose.

Bose had found a new way to derive Planck's equation describing black-body radiation. But Bose did this without assuming that light behaved as a wave at all! He dealt entirely in terms of particles, treating light as a gas of photons, a 'quantum gas', but he did so using a new kind of statistical law.

Einstein had always been intrigued by statistical relationships. The early work on Brownian motion and the work on stimulated emission, as well as his lesser-known studies of things like specific heat, had all used statistical techniques. Einstein took up the idea presented to him by Bose (after first translating Bose's paper, which had been written in English, into German and getting it published), and refined it, applying it to other problems. The new statistics became known as 'Bose–Einstein statistics', and the kind of particles that are (like photons) described by Bose–Einstein statistics are now known as bosons. The statistics apply to particles which, like photons, are not conserved – you make more photons, by the billion, whenever you switch a light on. It was Bose's work, and Einstein's extension of it, that finally established the reality of photons in the minds of physicists; and it was just over a year later that the word 'photon' was coined, in a paper published in 1926, written by the American Gilbert Lewis.

A different kind of statistics apply to particles in the quantum world that *are* conserved (like electrons; the number of electrons in the Universe stays the same, and you can only make an electron if you make its antimatter counterpart, a positron, as well). They were developed soon after, by Enrico Fermi and Paul Dirac. They are known as Fermi–Dirac statistics, and the particles they apply to are called fermions.

One of the implications of the new statistics was that if waves could be treated as particles, then particles could be treated as waves. Einstein was already tinkering with this idea, in the second half of 1924, when the French physicist Paul Langevin sent him a copy of the thesis submitted by Louis de Broglie for his Ph.D. De Broglie was suggesting that electrons could be treated as waves; Langevin wasn't sure if this was a stroke of genius, or completely insane. Einstein said that it was certainly not insane, and de Broglie got his Ph.D. He also got a major plug for his idea from Einstein, who referred to it in glowing terms in a paper he published in 1925. This approval from the greatest living scientist was enough to ensure that the idea of electron waves got off to a flying start; it was important enough to win de Broglie the Nobel prize for physics in 1929. In fact, though, if de Broglie hadn't come up with the idea just when he did, it is clear that Einstein would probably have come up with something similar, as a consequence of the development of Bose–Einstein statistics, before the end of 1925.

But that, as far as Einstein's original contributions to science were concerned, was it. As quantum physics developed into a complete, consistent (but very strange!) theory in the late 1920s, Einstein became increasingly alienated from the way physics was going. Ideas that he had godfathered, including the statistical treatment of quantum events like the emission of radiation, and the uncertainty implicit in the wave–particle duality, disturbed him more and more, and he made his famous comment that he could not believe that 'God plays dice' with the Universe. Einstein's own interests turned to a premature, and largely futile, attempt to develop a unified field theory, explaining gravity and electromagnetism in one package.

By the time he was 50, Einstein's major contributions to science were all behind him, though he did play an invaluable role as a critic of the new quantum theory, keeping its developers, such as Niels Bohr, on their toes by always being ready to jump in and point out any faults in the logic of their arguments. This would lead to one last memorable idea in physics, albeit one that didn't turn out as Einstein hoped.

In the 1920s, in spite of growing signs of trouble in the outside world (in which Einstein was actively involved as a pacifist) and the tedium of attending official functions (which he described as 'feeding time at the zoo'), Einstein at first had a secure and happy home life in Berlin. Ilse married in 1924, leaving Margot, Elsa and Albert as a close-knit domestic unit. He had his violin and his sailing for recreation, and by the early 1930s a summer home near the village of Caputh, a few miles from Potsdam, where he could sail his boat on the Havelsee. But he had also had another bout of serious illness in 1928, and proved too difficult a patient for Elsa (now in her fifties) to cope with unaided. At this point the 32-year-old Helen Dukas joined the household as, as she put it, 'chief cook and bottle washer' – a girl Friday, in slightly more modern parlance. She stayed with Einstein until he died, increasingly taking over the protective role from Elsa as time passed.

In 1930, Einstein made his first visit to California, where he was appointed a visiting Professor at Caltech (the California Institute of Technology), and was invited to return every year during the winter months. In May the following year he was in Oxford, where he was offered a research fellowship at Christ Church, with an annual payment of £400 on condition that he visited the college for a few weeks every summer. In Berlin, he was allowed to come and go as he pleased, wasn't really expected to lay any more scientific golden eggs, and could go off sailing at Caputh whenever he liked. But as the political situation in Germany deteriorated, and the Nazis became more powerful, there was a plot afoot to encourage Einstein to move to America permanently.

The plotter was Abraham Flexner, who planned to establish a new centre of scientific research, and was head-hunting top scientists to kick-start the enterprise. In 1932, he visited Caltech and discussed the idea with Robert Millikan, who was now running the institute. Millikan had his own hopes that Einstein would make his relationship with Caltech into a full-time position, but made the mistake of pointing out Einstein's obvious desirability as a figurehead to Flexner, thereby losing any chance of getting Einstein to settle in California. A few weeks later, Flexner visited Einstein in Oxford, told him of his plans, and said that if Einstein ever felt the inclination, he could write his own ticket to join the fledgling institute.

Einstein was intrigued, not so much at the thought of a permanent move but at adding another string to his bow. A couple of months later, Flexner visited the Einsteins in Caputh, and a deal was struck. Einstein would join the new Institute for Advanced Study, which would be based in Princeton, in the autumn of 1933, and would then divide his time largely between Berlin and Princeton. But things didn't work out that way.

On 10 December 1932, Albert and Elsa left

Germany for their annual visit to Caltech. On 30 January 1933, Adolf Hitler came to power in Germany. Hated by the Nazis as a pacifist and a Jew, Einstein could never return as long as they held power. His house was ransacked, copies of his books were burned in public along with those of other Jewish intellectuals, and he was accused of being a Communist agent. After his winter in California, Einstein did return to Europe, but not to Germany; he visited Oxford once again, and the Belgian seaside resort of Le Coq sur Mer, where he astonished the world by publicly proclaiming, in July 1933, that the Nazi threat was so great that, even as a long-time pacifist, he would be willing to take up arms against the threat in order to preserve European civilization. On 7 October he set sail once again, for the last time, to America, where he settled in Princeton with his entourage.

In America, Einstein was famous for being famous, and he certainly helped to get the Institute for Advanced Study established as a prestigious research centre. But he achieved nothing more in the way of real science, and in his private life, after settling in America, he did only two interesting things. The first was to write (at the suggestion of Eugene Wigner and Leo Szilard) a letter to President Roosevelt urging him to take seriously the idea of building a nuclear bomb (though Einstein was never actively involved in the Manhattan Project, and later came to deeply regret his action); the second was to turn down the offer of the presidency of the young state of Israel. Elsa died in 1936, and from then until he died, on 12 April 1955, Einstein was guarded by Helen Dukas. Even after his death, Dukas jealously (and over-protectively) guarded the Einstein archive, and protected his image from what she regarded as unseemly interest, so that it was only in the 1990s (Dukas died in 1982) that many details of his private life (including the birth of his illegitimate daughter) came to light.

Just a year before Elsa died, though, Einstein was involved in one last bright idea, which has repercussions at the cutting-edge of research in quantum physics today. Still critical of the quantum theory, and trying to devise a logical argument which would prove that it was wrong, he dreamed up (together with his colleagues Nathan Rosen and Boris Podolsky) a 'thought experiment' which became known as the EPR paradox.

Their paper was published in 1935, and highlighted the strange feature of the quantum world known as non-locality. Translating their account into slightly different terms, we can look at the problem in terms of an atomic nucleus which spits out two particles, simultaneously, in opposite directions. One is an electron, the other is a positron, but we do not know which is which. One of the features which Einstein found abhorrent in the standard version of quantum theory (often known as the Copenhagen Interpretation, because it was partly developed in that city) is that the particles themselves do not know what they are until they are measured, or interact with something. They exist as a mixture of the two possible states (a superposition of states) up to that time. But they cannot both be in the same state – they cannot both be the same kind of particle, in this version of the experiment. So the moment that you measure particle A, and find out that it is, say, an electron, particle B must instantaneously become a positron, with no uncertainty about its state, no matter how far away it is. *Neither* particle exists in *either* state, only as the superposition, until it is measured, or interacts with another particle. What you measure to be an electron was not an electron 'all the time', but only settled into that state at the moment it was observed, while the other particle instantaneously settled into the other state at the same time. Something which Einstein called a 'spooky action at a distance' seems to reach out across space (not just faster than light, but literally instantaneously) to tell the other particle how to behave. It is obvious why this is called non-locality: the influence could hardly be less local.

To Einstein and his colleagues, this was proof that the quantum theory was flawed. They never imagined that the experiment would be carried out; the logic of the argument was good enough for them. But in the 1950s and 1960s, through the work of David Bohm and John Bell, it became clear that such an experiment really could be carried out. In the 1980s it was done, several times (actually using photons in different quantum states, not electrons and positrons). The result? Non-locality was seen to be at work. The spooky action at a distance really does exist, and for once Einstein was wrong. Perhaps it's just as well that he didn't live to see the experiment carried out, though as a good scientist (like Millikan) he would surely have accepted its results.

Afterword

Einstein would have been disappointed to learn that non-locality really is a feature of the quantum world. But he would surely have been delighted that this discovery has led to a rethink about the nature of quantum reality, and to the removal of the Copenhagen Interpretation – which he loathed – from its position of pre-eminence. There are several other respectable interpretations of quantum theory now vying for that top slot, and trying to get around the puzzle of how quantum entities can exist in a strange superposition of states, only collapsing into one definite state or another when they are observed. Just how this might be achieved is far from clear, but the meaning of quantum reality is today the subject of a debate more lively than at any time since Bohr and Einstein argued about it in the 1930s.

The sexiest area of physics today, at least in the public eye, is undoubtedly the theory of the Big Bang and the question of when and how the Universe as we know it came into existence. Present-day cosmology is based almost entirely on Einstein's general theory of relativity, which describes all of space and all of time. When Einstein first looked at his equations in this context in 1916 and 1917, he found that they required space to be expanding (or possibly contracting, but definitely not standing still). He thought this so ridiculous that he introduced an extra term into the equations, a 'cosmological constant', to hold the Universe still. By the end of the 1920s, astronomers had discovered that the Universe really is expanding, and Einstein later described his 'correction' to the equations as the 'biggest blunder' of his career. The same equations that describe the expanding Universe also describe the way that matter can collapse to form black holes.

At the other extreme of physics, in the world of the very small, the Holy Grail of science is to find a unified field theory. Einstein was way ahead of his time in trying to do this in the 1930s and 1940s, not least because when he started on the quest nobody knew of the existence of two more forces of nature, in addition to gravity and electromagnetism. These are the so-called strong and weak nuclear forces, which operate only over distances comparable to the size of an atomic nucleus. Einstein's quest for a unified field theory was not misguided, but premature – he simply didn't have enough information to begin to make progress.

So where does he stand in the pantheon of physics? Comparisons are odious, but few people would argue against the claim that Isaac Newton was the greatest of then all. In a foreword to a twentieth-century edition of Newton's *Optics*, Einstein himself wrote:

Nature was to him an open book, whose letters he could read without effort. The conceptions which he used to reduce the material of experience to order seemed to flow spontaneously from experience itself, from the beautiful experiments which he ranged in order like playthings and described with an affectionate wealth of detail. In one person, he combined the experimenter, the theorist, the mechanic and, not least, the artist in exposition. He stands before us strong, certain, and alone; his joy in creation and his minute precision are evident in every word and every figure.

Einstein wasn't much of an experimenter, but otherwise that would rate pretty well as his own epitaph. Number two to Newton in the physics rankings is surely a position he would be proud to hold – though he might have to share that number two slot with Richard Feynman.

A brief history of science

All science is either physics or stamp collecting.

Ernest Rutherford

c. 2000 BC   First phase of construction at Stonehenge, an early observatory.

430 BC   Democritus teaches that everything is made of atoms.

c. 330 BC   Aristotle teaches that the Universe is made of concentric spheres, centred on the Earth.

300 BC   Euclid gathers together and writes down the mathematical knowledge of his time.

265 BC   Archimedes discovers his principle of buoyancy while having a bath.

c. 235 BC   Eratosthenes of Cyrene calculates the size of the Earth with commendable accuracy.

AD 79   Pliny the Elder dies while

studying an eruption of Mount Vesuvius.

400   The term 'chemistry' is used for the first time, by scholars in Alexandria.

c. 1020   Alhazen, the greatest scientist of the so-called Dark Ages, explains the workings of lenses and parabolic mirrors.

1054   Chinese astronomers observe a supernova; the remnant is visible today as the Crab Nebula.

1490   Leonardo da Vinci studies the capillary action of liquids.

1543   In his book *De revolutionibus*, Nicolaus Copernicus places the Sun, not the Earth, at the centre of the Solar System. Andreas Vesalius studies human anatomy in a scientific way.

c. 1550   The reflecting telescope, and later the refracting telescope, pioneered by Leonard Digges.

1572	Tycho Brahe observes a supernova.
1580	Prospero Alpini realizes that plants come in two sexes.
1596	Botanical knowledge is summarized in John Gerrard's *Herbal*.
1608	Hans Lippershey's invention of a refracting telescope is the first for which there is firm evidence.
1609–19	Johannes Kepler publishes his laws of planetary motion.
1610	Galileo Galilei observes the moons of Jupiter through a telescope.
1628	William Harvey publishes his discovery of the circulation of the blood.
1643	Mercury barometer invented by Evangelista Torricelli.
1656	Christiaan Huygens correctly identifies the rings of Saturn,

and invents the pendulum clock.

1662   The law relating the pressure and volume of a gas discovered by Robert Boyle, and named after him.

1665   Robert Hooke describes living cells.

1668   A functional reflecting telescope is made by Isaac Newton, unaware of Digges's earlier work.

1673   Antony van Leeuwenhoeck reports his discoveries with the microscope to the Royal Society.

1675   Ole Roemer measures the speed of light by timing eclipses of the moons of Jupiter.

1683   Van Leeuwenhoeck observes bacteria.

1687   Publication of Newton's

	Principia, which includes his law of gravitation.
1705	Edmond Halley publishes his prediction of the return of the comet that now bears his name.
1737	Carl Linnaeus publishes his classification of plants.
1749	Georges Louis Leclerc, Comte de Buffon, defines a species in the modern sense.
1758	Halley's Comet returns, as predicted.
1760	John Michell explains earthquakes.
1772	Carl Scheele discovers oxygen; Joseph Priestley independently discovers it two years later.
1773	Pierre de Laplace begins his work on refining planetary orbits. When asked by Napoleon why there was no mention of God in his scheme, Laplace replied, 'I have no

need of that hypothesis.'

1783   John Michell is the first person to suggest the existence of 'dark stars' – now known as black holes.

1789   Antoine Lavoisier publishes a table of thirty-one chemical elements.

1796   Edward Jenner carries out the first inoculation, against smallpox.

1798   Henry Cavendish determines the mass of the Earth.

1802   Thomas Young publishes his first paper on the wave theory of light.
        Jean-Baptiste Lamarck invents the term 'biology'.

1803   John Dalton proposes the atomic theory of matter.

1807   Humphrey Davy discovers sodium and potassium, and goes on to find several other elements.

1811	Amedeo Avogadro proposes the law that gases contain equal numbers of molecules under the same conditions.
1816	Augustin Fresnel develops his version of the wave theory of light.
1826	First photograph from nature obtained by Nicéphore Niépce.
1828	Friedrich Wöhler synthesizes an organic compound (urea) from inorganic ingredients.
1830	Publication of the first volume of Charles Lyell's *Principles of Geology*.
1831	Michael Faraday and Joseph Henry discover electromagnetic induction. Charles Darwin sets sail on the *Beagle*.
1837	Louis Agassiz coins the term 'ice age' (*die Eiszeit*).
1842	Christian Doppler describes

the effect that now bears his name.

1849 Hippolyte Fizeau measures the speed of light to within 5 per cent of the modern value.

1851 Jean Foucault uses his eponymous pendulum to demonstrate the rotation of the Earth.

1857 Publication of Darwin's *Origin of Species*. Coincidentally, Gregor Mendel begins his experiments with pea breeding.

1864 James Clerk Maxwell formulates equations describing all electric and magnetic phenomena, and shows that light is an electromagnetic wave.

1868 Jules Janssen and Norman Lockyer identify helium from its lines in the Sun's spectrum.

1871 Dmitri Mendeleyev predicts

that 'new' elements will be found to fit the gaps in his periodic table.

1887   Experiment carried out by Albert Michelson and Edward Morley finds no evidence for the existence of an 'aether'.

1895   X-rays discovered by Wilhelm Röntgen. Sigmund Freud begins to develop psychoanalysis.

1896   Antoine Becquerel discovers radioactivity.

1897   Electron identified by Joseph Thomson.

1898   Marie and Pierre Curie discover radium.

1900   Max Planck explains how electromagnetic radiation is absorbed and emitted as quanta. Various biologists rediscover Medel's principles of genetics and heredity.

1903   First powered and controlled

flight in an aircraft heavier
than air, by Orville Wright.

1905   Einstein's special theory of
        relativity published.

1908   Hermann Minkowski shows
        that the special theory of
        relativity can be elegantly
        explained in geometrical terms
        if time is the fourth dimension.

1909   First use of the word 'gene',
        by Wilhelm Johannsen.

1912   Discovery of cosmic rays by
        Victor Hess. Alfred Wegener
        proposes the idea of
        continental drift, which led in
        the 1960s to the theory of
        plate tectonics.

1913   Discovery of the ozone layer
        by Charles Fabry.

1914   Ernest Rutherford discovers
        the proton, a name he coins in
        1919.

1915   Einstein presents his general
        theory of relativity to the

Prussian Academy of Sciences.

1916   Karl Schwarzschild shows that the general theory of relativity predicts the existence of what are now called black holes.

1919   Arthur Eddington and others observe the bending of starlight during a total eclipse of the Sun, and so confirm the accuracy of the general theory of relativity. Rutherford splits the atom.

1923   Louis de Broglie suggests that electrons can behave as waves.

1926   Enrico Fermi and Paul Dirac discover the statistical rules which govern the behaviour of quantum particles such as electrons.

1927   Werner Heisenberg develops the uncertainty principle.

1928   Alexander Fleming discovers penicillin.

1929   Edwin Hubble discovers that
            the Universe is expanding.

1930s   Linus Pauling explains
            chemistry in terms of quantum
            physics.

1932   Neutron discovered by James
            Chadwick.

1937   Grote Reber builds the first
            radio telescope.

1942   First controlled nuclear
            reaction achieved by Enrico
            Fermi and others.

1940s   George Gamow, Ralph
            Alpher and Robert Herman
            develop the Big Bang theory of
            the origin of the Universe.

1948   Richard Feynman extends
            quantum theory by developing
            quantum electrodynamics.

1951   Francis Crick and James
            Watson work out the helix
            structure of DNA, using X-ray
            results obtained by Rosalind
            Franklin.

1957   Fred Hoyle, together with William Fowler and Geoffrey and Margaret Burbidge, explains how elements are synthesized inside stars. The laser is devised by Gordon Gould. Launch of first artificial satellite, *Sputnik 1.*

1960   Jacques Monod and Francis Jacob identify messenger RNA.

1961   First part of the genetic code cracked by Marshall Nirenberg.

1963   Discovery of quasars by Maarten Schmidt.

1964   W.D. Hamilton explains altruism in terms of what is now called sociobiology.

1965   Arno Penzias and Robert Wilson discover the cosmic background radiation left over from the Big Bang.